A FREIGHT TRAIN IN MY BRAIN

SURVIVING SCHIZOPHRENIA

by
Michael W. Gregg

AuthorHouse™
1663 Liberty Drive, Suite 200
Bloomington, IN 47403
www.authorhouse.com
Phone: 1-800-839-8640

First published by AuthorHouse 7/19/2007

ISBN: 978-1-4259-9251-4 (e)
ISBN: 978-1-4259-9250-7 (sc)

Library of Congress Control Number: 2007904040

Printed in the United States of America
Bloomington, Indiana

This book is printed on acid-free paper.

This Book is
Lovingly and Gratefully Dedicated
To My Mother

CONTENTS

Chapter	Title	Page

I

SURVIVING SCHIZOPHRENIA

Janos is a small place. A one-hotel town where the frequent trucker makes a pit stop and the occasional traveler just pauses as he passes through. It was a bit noisy their first night there but they didn't care. They had what they needed - a room without a view, a heater, plenty of blankets and a king-size bed. Oh, and a snowy, three-channel TV with no remote control.

Lena and he shared three wonderful nights in Janos loving, laughing and eating Mexican chicharrones all night every night. What did they care - they had hot running water, clean towels and good wine to help keep them company. The strawberries he put in the cooler had gone bad because he forgot the ice but the cream and the salt-free crackers they had were delicious.

For him, it had been about three years and for her at least six. She proudly admitted there had only been two men in her life and at age 32, to him, that's quite an accomplishment. Her first husband was abusive in every way but physical. While she was pregnant that bastard would leave her hungry and cold. Even after Jessica was born she walked for miles with baby in hand to her in-laws to ask for help. They were just as cruel and turned her away at the door. She finally went back home to live with her parents who naturally took her in. The day Barco showed up at the door, Lena's father ran him off at gunpoint. Being the coward that he is, he has never returned. He obviously didn't give a damn about his own daughter. Lena divorced him and to Billy's good fortune they met, married and found themselves in each other's arms at The Hacienda Hotel in Janos, Mexico - a one-intersection, two-restaurant town

What were they doing there? Well, Billy's wife is Mexican and they couldn't wait for her VISA to be approved so they planned and scheduled a church wedding and VISA or no VISA they got married. What has all this to do with schizophrenia? Well, Billy's road to successfully surviving the illness was a long and difficult one. I hope you find it interesting and appreciate the experiences he endured to beat schizophrenia. Perhaps his experiences coping with it can offer a bit of inspiration to someone dealing with it now.

II

CHILDHOOD

His family was poor and whether they were aware of it or not, he didn't know. Whether they even cared, he couldn't recall. Social classes were very blurred in their small community. They ran with the rich as easily as they ran with the poor. Grants was a small mining town in northern New Mexico. "The Uranium Capital of the World," townspeople bragged. Those who lived there worked in the mines, were related to, or knew someone who worked in them. If you graduated from the local high school chances were you would become a miner like your father or uncle or friend.

The front door of their little, green, five-room brick house was 10 yards from the legendary Route 66 and the back door was at about 100 yards away from the ATS&F railroad tracks. They had one restroom, one tub, one sink and one table for all 13 of Billy's family members.

How they were ever satisfied at the table or ever got ready to catch the bus for school on time one will never know. An even greater mystery, to this day, is how most of them survived that environment.

Living on US Highway 66 made many smart businessmen rich. His father tried to tap into that gold mine. He built a string of one-bedroom apartments, which he rented to supplement his miner's income.

Freddie, Billy's older brother, and he slept in room 5. One night Billy was there alone and it was cold. There was no heat and no electricity in the apartments, so he rigged up a source of heat for himself. He ran an electrical cord with a light bulb from the main house to room 5. He tied the cord to a ceiling light fixture and placed the light under his blanket making a lighted tent for himself and fell asleep. The next morning, he woke up to a burning cotton mattress. Fortunately, only the mattress and blankets burned. The mattress smoldered for days and days out back.

For whatever reason, by the time Billy was a young teenager the apartments were no longer being rented. Maybe it was because renters kept stealing the blankets and sheets and everything that wasn't tied down.

In the 60's, gas was very inexpensive. The family could travel from Grants to Albuquerque, about 75 miles, on

$2.00 worth of gas. And, they often did. Not all of them, but most of them would squeeze in the family station wagon on many weekends and go to Grandma's house in the Five Points area in Albuquerque. One weekend, as they were leaving Albuquerque they left Debra behind and didn't realize it until they were well on their way home.

III

<u>HIS FATHER</u>

His father was not always a loving, caring parent. He was often the typical abusive, alcoholic miner. With Billy, he was only verbally abusive. But to his older brother and two younger brothers he was also physically abusive.

Billy remembers one occasion at the dinner table after everyone had finished eating. His younger brother, A.J., was sitting in a chair next to their very drunk father. For reasons known only to him, their father grabbed A.J. by the hair and banged his head repeatedly against the brick wall behind him. Billy couldn't understand what A.J. did to piss him off that way. It couldn't have been anything too serious because A.J. was only 11 years old at the time. Billy went to the living room and told his mother what his father was doing and she said, "Tell your dad I want to talk to A.J." He reluctantly let him go.

To Freddie, he was especially mean. As the oldest son, his father expected him to be perfect. But, Freddie did what he wanted and generally just came and went as he pleased. He had a very wild streak in him. At one time his father had a green '62 Chevy pickup that smoked like a train, but Freddie drove it like it was a hotrod anyway. He didn't care that it wouldn't respond he just drove it to the ground. The truck belonged to his father and that's why Freddie deliberately abused it the way he did.

One day he and a couple of his friends decided to ditch school and they went to Mount Taylor - a twenty-minute dirt-road drive from Grants. Regardless of the road conditions, Freddie loved to speed. That day he found out that driving fast on a gravel road is very dangerous. His father's newly-purchased, tan, '57 Chevy fishtailed and flipped over a couple of times down a shallow cliff. Fortunately, the truck landed right side up. Except for a few bumps and bruises his buddies suffered, no one was seriously hurt. His father, however, was devastated. Seeing his new truck all banged up made him so angry he couldn't see straight - and he took it out on everyone.

Freddie loved football and he played for the Grants High School Pirates his Junior and Senior years. That day, Freddie left the truck at home and went to football practice just to be out of his father's space when he came home. Billy didn't know if it was for ditching or for wrecking the truck, but his father went for Freddie in the truck and yanked him out of practice, uniform and all.

On the way home, in the pick-up, Billy sat between his father and Freddie. His father reached over him and fiercely backhanded Freddie again and again. He must have loosened a couple of Freddie's teeth because his mouth and his dad's hand were bleeding. When they got home the lectures began. All that night and for days to follow he hovered over Fred - waiting for him to make another mistake. There's no telling what he would have done to him.

On winter nights Billy and his older brother slept in Room 1 because it had a wood stove. They, however, were too lazy to get up in the early morning to put another log in the fire. So, their father would come from the main house to do that and in the process, chew Freddie out.

Much of the time it seemed that their father was not around. He worked a lot of swing and graveyard shifts and during the day he slept. When he was home, and awake, he was very intimidating. On weekends he was often passed out in his bedroom. Many times when Billy was with him, his father went into bars and left him sitting in the truck for hours. Occasionally, he would bring him a bag of peanuts.

Physically, his father was not a big person but he made up for his size with his aggressive nature. Being a miner he was extremely strong and had a deep forceful voice. When he wanted to say something there was no doubt he would get his point across.

He came from a family of miners. Miguel and Juan, his two older brothers, died in or because of the mines. Samuel, his younger brother, was about 36 when he became crippled for life in a mining accident. His father would proudly declare, "I spent 29 years 7 months underground breathing dirt to keep us fed and clothed and a roof over our heads. I don't have to be your father - I do it because I want to, not because I have to. I can do anything I want, I can go where I want and do what I want."

Behind their little green house and in front of the corral that housed the neighbor's (Jerry) horses, there was a wrecking yard that occupied more than half the field between their house and the railroad tracks. The cars were lined up in such a way that Ray, Clyde, JB, Richard and Billy often played tag, jumping from car to car. Some times they broke the metal trim off the sides of cars and made swords to compete in their own form of medieval sword fights. Billy has a 6-inch scar on the right side of his chest that attests to their battles.

On cool nights they gathered between cars, started a campfire, roasted wieners and potatoes and invited the neighborhood schoolgirls to join them - Linda and Stacy were especially welcomed.

IV

COMRADES IN CRIME

Billy and his neighbor, Ray, were terrors to the whole town. Ray was 4 years his senior but they were fearless comrades and at 12 what did he know or care about age differences anyway. If Ray got an idea to create some mischief Billy would not hesitate to join him. And, Ray was always looking to cause trouble somewhere or to someone. For example, when either of them needed parts for their bicycles (which they couldn't afford) they stole them. Those bikes provided transportation for their many adventures.

Ray always carried a bottle opener with which they popped the top off any soft drink in those old-fashioned coke machines. Using a straw or a cup, they drank as much soda of whatever flavor they wanted until they were full. If they needed money, Ray knew where Jerry, his older, hard-working brother, hid his hard-earned dollars and would raid his stash. Jerry, of course, would get furious and physically beat the hell out of Ray. But he could take a beating better than anyone Billy ever knew. After all, he had survived his mother's beatings time and again.

When they had nothing to do, Ray could come up with the sneakiest schemes to have a good time. One day they were trying to figure out how to impress Linda. "She loves horses," Ray told Billy, "but if we take Jerry's that will be the end of me. I know where there are some horses that don't belong to anyone. We can go get them and take her for a ride if we want." So off they went past Mount Taylor Park on Old 66 for those horses. It took them all day to corral them because they had to chase them half way up the mesa to catch them. They came down Old 66 steering the horses with their makeshift bridles thinking Linda was going to love this. They, however, didn't make it to her house - the police caught them first. "Where did you get these horses? Whose horses are they? What are you doing riding them into town? Who's your dad?" They asked Billy. They didn't even bother questioning Ray. They already knew him and immediately put him in the back seat of the police car. To this day Billy pictures Ray sitting back there pointing at him and laughing. Billy, however, had to stand there holding the horses until his mother came and slapped him across the face and asked him what the hell was he doing stealing horses. "Just you wait till your Dad gets home," she said.

The horses belonged to Mr. McDonald, the public school superintendent. Was he ever pissed when he showed up. "Where the hell did you cut my fence, you little bastard!" He screamed. "We didn't," Billy answered. "We separated the barbwires halfway up the mesa and pulled them through the fence." He then rode off on one horse and led the other one along behind him in the dark.

Ray was released in his father's custody and Billy was placed in a jail cell. There he sat on a cold, steel bunk bed for half the night, looking out onto old Route 66 through a basement window. His father, after his graveyard shift, either bailed him out or just picked him up. He doesn't know for sure which. They locked Billy up in that cell just to scare him straight because he was only 12 years old at the time. It must have worked. Considering what his father could have done to him, he let him off easy. His father thought it was funny, and at the time he needed something humorous in his life because he had recently lost his two older brothers.

Ray's rebellious nature was probably a reaction to his mother's abusive discipline. Instead of trying to teach him how to stay out of trouble she inadvertently drove him to deliberately commit more. As punishment she forced him to make adobes in the blistering heat or in the freezing cold - for hours on end and for no other reason than just plain old meanness. Billy knew this because the adobes lay there, unused, for years and years. Whenever

Ray did something wrong or whenever she felt like it, to the backyard to make adobes he would go.

Ray's father, well, he was as passive as any father could be. His father was completely intimidated and afraid of that mean old lady. Billy can still hear that high-pitched shrill of her scream, "RAY, RAY, RAY," and never "JERRY, JERRY, JERRY," or "CHUKIE, CHUKIE, CHUKIE" (his younger brother).

Her anger toward Ray may have been related to a daughter born with polio who needed extensive care. Maybe she took her bitterness out on Ray. On the other hand, he very often gave her reason to punish him. Ray was always looking for trouble and always finding it - at home or on the streets.

The last Billy heard about Ray was that he had been imprisoned for raping two 50-year-old ladies who he threatened to rape again if they said anything. He is now in a New Mexico State Prison and as far as Billy knows, Ray's a hardened career criminal. Now why the hell he is there and Billy is here when they both come from essentially the same background is a good question that's probably beyond anyone to answer.

V

TENDER FATHERLY MOMENTS

There were a few tender times Billy shared with his father. Sometimes, when he was sober, he would hug him and lift him up in the air. This was so peculiar a behavior Billy didn't know how to accept it so he would gently push his father away. His expression of fatherly love was so rare that on those occasions Billy wasn't sure what it was or what he was doing.

Billy recalls that his father loved to take his sons deer hunting. He was a very good hunter because he knew where to find deer. For example, he knew there were always deer near an old mining camp where he had worked as a young man. During one hunting season he, Freddie, and Billy went to the Zuni Mountains very early in the morning. As the sun rose on the way up the old mountain road, they turned the bend and near the abandoned mineshaft he spotted several bucks. He quickly picked one out, shot from the truck and bang - they had one!

Late that evening, his father and Freddie went back to the Zuni Mountains and shot a second deer. There had been no checkpoint early that morning and his father did not expect there would be one late that night, but he was wrong. The problem was that the second deer wasn't tagged because they didn't buy a license for it. That little venture cost him a late-night appearance before a judge, $300, both deer, and his 30-30 Winchester rifle.

Everyone knew him not only as a mean father but also as a mean man in general. He could be courageous too. One evening there was a wildly barking, rabid dog that had everybody in the neighborhood running scared - especially the kids. Someone called the dog pound and the dogcatchers came out but were too frightened to get close to the dog. The dog had rabies. It, however, just kept coming closer and closer to the little green brick house until it was under the family yellow Dodge. Billy's father took control. Unlike the story in To Kill a Mockingbird where Atticus Finch shoots the rabid dog, Billy's father took the pole with the rope attached to the end of it and collared the dog. He picked it up and tossed it in the dogcatcher's cage. In a fit of anger, he then ran off the cowardly dogcatchers.

There was another incident where Billy recalls seeing his father's courage. Behind the family home and beyond his basketball goal, was a wrecking yard. There, the neighborhood kids would often take the car seats out of the cars and jump on them. On one occasion, Billy could hear a rattling noise every time he jumped down on the seat. He reported this to his father. He came, turned the car seat upside down and sure enough, there laid a rattle snake. His father immediately and efficiently killed it with a shovel.

His father loved to take his sons with him to his job. He took Freddie and Billy so that they could see and experience for themselves what it was like to be a miner. Billy went into one of the mines and quickly learned how dangerous it was. He often wonders how his father survived 29 years and 7 months in those mines. One weekend he shut down the mine because it was too dangerous to work in it. That very weekend the mineshaft caved in.

Once his father could no longer pass the required physical and was "thrown out" of the big mines he resorted to working for small, independent mining companies by signing waivers relieving them of all responsibility for his health.

The only time he ever punished Billy, he deserved it. One evening Ray and Billy were riding Chocolate (the tamest of all Jerry's horses) and as his father drove in the yard his headlights caught the exact moment Chocolate bucked them both off. Not only did the horse buck Billy off, his father kicked his butt several times with his steel-toed boot. He told Billy "that will be the last time I ever want to see you ride any of those horses." And it was the last time he saw him, but not the last time he rode them.

VI

<u>OUT OF CONTROL</u>

What drove his father to do some of the things he did is a mystery. There were times when he was completely out of control. In order to keep his family fed and clothed he had to work. To be able to work in the mines, he was required to pass a physical. On one occasion Dr. Gonzales couldn't give him a clean bill of health. That, of course, meant his father couldn't work, so, he threatened the doctor with a knife. There were other incidents which revealed just how wild this man could get.

Billy knew of one other pocketknife incident even more serious that could have cost a complete stranger his life. Ruth, one of Billy's sisters, was working for a boss who refused to pay her what she was owed. She reported this to her father. Her father immediately drove to Ruth's place of employment and verbally threatened her boss while holding a pocketknife to his throat. The $600 check her boss issued cleared the bank without incident.

As far as Billy knows, his father never physically abused any of his 7 daughters, but there were things he made them do they would never forget. He once met and befriended a complete stranger at a bar and together they made plans to go partying. Billy's father went home, picked Debra up, took her to the stranger's trailer and left her there babysitting the stranger's children. Eventually, his father went home, forgetting all about Debra. Imagine how frightening that was for her. The "stranger" staggered into the trailer at dawn and found Debra sitting on the couch petrified and crying. He had actually left her alone with that stranger. Fortunately the man drove her home without incident.

His father had his favorites. Billy avoided the man as much as possible so he didn't know why he was on his good side along with Ruth and Janice. Laura, the oldest, was just as rebellious as Freddie. She and her father never saw eye to eye on anything. As far back as Billy can remember they were always arguing. Day and night arguing - never a moment of peace between the two.

His natural disposition, most of the time, was just pure and plain old anger. Why? Probably because he was living a very hard life, spending much of it underground sucking dirt and supporting 11 kids. But it was his own doing. He and his wife, from the moment they met, decided to have as many kids as they could. No matter the economics, no matter how hard things got, no matter who got hurt, no matter anything - they were determined to live out their lives the way they had planned and they surely did.

VII

<u>HIS MOTHER</u>

His mother, on the other hand, held things together for them. Keeping some sort of sanity in the house was an enormous job, but she did it. From the oldest to the youngest and everyone in between she held them together. Cooking, cleaning, sweeping, and washing - whatever needed to be done she would do it. The only thing she couldn't do enough of was to nurture each of the eleven children adequately.   And, that was understandable. There were so many. So, they had to do it for themselves. Billy did without, like everyone else.

His mother was overwhelmed with 10 other kids to take time for him personally. She always had a baby in her arms, household responsibilities, and a mean, argumentative husband to contend with. He imagines the rest of his siblings must have felt the same way at some time. Survival, without a mother's love, was a personal thing and each of them dealt with it in their own way. In other words, they dealt with it, and they dealt without it too.

Billy doesn't blame his mother for not being able to love him adequately because she gave what she could and as much as she could. She was as loving as was possible considering the circumstances. After all, 9 kids did survive without being scarred severely. Freddie, after serving in the military, was never the same spirited, adventurous, rebellious person and took his own life at age 28. A.J. died at 17 as a result of a motorcycle accident - he was traveling too fast over a gravel road on a borrowed motorcycle. Although, some of his siblings would disagree about how well their scars have healed and how well they successfully function today.

VIII

HIGH SCHOOL YEARS

Success, as we all know, is generally measured financially. What one drives, where one lives or how far one has advanced in a career. But who is to say that overcoming tremendous odds to simply maintain a functioning level of sanity is not as much of an achievement as acquiring wealth or prestige or fame. After all, how much can one fit into a garage, how much does one feed a career before it ends? But finding a way to maintain ones own sanity, to someone who knows what it is to live without it, can alone be a successful accomplishment. It's a precious fleeting entity to some and completely taken for granted by others.

Billy has experienced both - success in its more familiar form, and in an indistinct form. To him the latter is much more valuable. But the former, on the surface at least, is more gratifying. As a high school student he was an athlete, and a very good one. Like everyone, he had one goal in mind - to be the best. It took him three years to do it but he did it successfully.

As a Sophomore he tried every sport until he finally found the one at which he could excel. Football was much too aggressive and eating dirt wasn't for him. Besides, he didn't have the size or the inclination to succeed at it. He was too slow for track. Baseball was not that popular. Tennis was not that well organized. There was not even a soccer team to join. Wrestling required too much training and the benefit wasn't worth it. So basketball it was. He could train on his own, in his own backyard. He could find a pickup game practically anywhere, anytime. He could use his leadership skills to their maximum, and the reward for winning was definitely worth seeking.

He was a starter on the Junior varsity team during his Sophomore year - but they won their share of games. Occasionally, he even got to play in a varsity game but not enough to earn a letter. The varsity team lost more games than they won that year. But he knew that if he stuck with it he could definitely play regularly as a Junior. So, he studied the game from the bench and played hard when he got the chance to show his skills.

The next year he earned a starting point guard position and never lost it. The team won 16 games and lost 13.

But more importantly, they won the games that counted. At the end of the year they beat the favored St Pius' Sartans in the district tournament and won their way into the State Tournament. At State they beat Tucumcari to advance to the second round. They took 4th place and got a taste of what it felt like to play at the highest level of competition in their class. They ended the year advancing further in the State Tournament than any other Grants team had ever gone.

They started their Senior year extremely confident. So confident that Billy promised the student body at the first pep rally they would finish the season 31 and 0 and come home with the State championship trophy. But the start of the season was mediocre at best. They were 8 and 4 before the Christmas break. They lost one district game at home to Aztec and three games in the double elimination tournament at the Roswell Invitational. Nevertheless, Billy was determined that the team would not lose another game during the season. Along the way, they won the Gallup Invitational and the District tournaments and had a 16-game winning streak going into the State Tournament. They won both the quarter-final and the semi-final games to advance into the final championship game. Their opponent was West Las Vegas who had knocked them out of the tournament the previous year and had a 27 and 0 winning streak coming into the final championship game. They were ranked No. 1 and Grants was ranked No. 2. Billy came 4 games short of his prediction. They finished the season with a 27 and 4 record and the state championship trophy.

He got a taste of true success and fame for a brief time. It felt great, and he left high school wanting more of the same.

IX

FROM HERO TO ZERO

Following high school Billy enrolled at New Mexico State University and went from hero to nobody in one summer. After high school, for some reason, he was never able to adjust to the change. He could not relate to either students or teachers. He felt removed and distant from whatever situation he faced. Friendships were difficult to make. In 4½ years of college he can't remember one person he came to know personally.

Although, he made the grades and completed his studies in time, there was always a feeling of estrangement that haunted him everywhere he went. He did everything with extreme caution - never allowing anyone to get close to him. Eventually, he even lost old friendships from Grants. He was unable to trust anyone. Old girlfriends with whom he had been somewhat intimate were now becoming strangers. He was unable to connect on a personal or social level with friends he had known and trusted for years. Social situations were impossible for him and he avoided them at all cost.

Throughout Billy's youth it never occurred to him that he might have a problem connecting with people. Being an athlete and somewhat popular he always had plenty of close female and male friends. The depth of his relationship with others always seemed comfortable, but looking back now there was no depth. All personal connections he had with friends, female or male, were extremely shallow.

The bond he had with his two closest friends, JC and Tommy, throughout his adolescence and young adult years, to him, felt perfectly normal - anyway, as normal as friendships can be at that age. But once he got to college those two relationships began to erode and by the time he finished college they were complete strangers to him. For two friends to grow apart or for one to mature faster than another is normal but for them to become foreigners to each other is abnormal, isn't it? Well that's the way all his old male friendships ended and for years and years he was never able to form new ones.

X

EARLY ADULT YEARS

As for female friends, well, the story is similar. One summer Billy kissed 35 different girls. Granted, it was the summer between his Junior and Senior years of high school and he had made it a mission to kiss as many girls as he could that summer - and he did. However, his inability to form any kind of a serious bond with any of these girls was typical of what happened to him throughout his early adult years. There were girlfriends that he dated for a few months, but, typically he was only able to develop a friendship at a very superficial level. He and Sally dated most of his Senior year and they kissed and hugged often but he was never able even to go steady with her. They went to the prom, high school dances, games, and concerts. They did a lot of things together and they even had an understanding that they would hook up sometime later in life but that never happened because he simply moved on. He dated Janelle in his

Junior year. The same thing happened - he moved on to another shallow friendship.

After high school there was Marie - this time things got a little more serious and they were engaged for a brief time. Again, he was unable to permanently bond with her or anyone else for that matter. They dated off and on for at least 5 years and he thought she was the right girl for him. Not so. She cheated on him with his best friend Tommy. On a holiday in Tommy's apartment, after partying for hours, she got up from his bed thinking he was passed out from the beer and the wine and the pot and climbed into Tommy's bed. Weeks later Billy vaguely remembered Tommy coming into their bedroom and telling Marie, "Come with me, he's passed out." Little by little he remembered what had happened that night and he finally realized what she and Tommy had done to him. He broke off their engagement sometime later and to this day he doesn't know if she realizes why.

In spite of the deep personal conflicts he was experiencing, after high school his sights were set extremely high. He studied hard and gradually discovered that architecture came naturally to him and he was good at it. So, he transferred to a school that offered an architectural program. There, he found the same kind of excitement in studying buildings as he had found in studying his point guard position from the bench. Here he was, again, loving what he was doing and doing it very well.

After transferring he graduated from a four-year program in two years and was off to seek his fame and fortune - completely unaware of his haunting affliction.

XI

A NEW CHALLENGE

Off to Denver Billy went where he found a job with Stone and Webster Engineering Corporation - a very big and very good engineering firm. He wasn't exactly sure what he wanted immediately, but that company offered him the opportunity to improve his skills and learn how buildings were put together. He worked there for two years as a structural design/drafter on hydroelectric and fossil fuel power plants. There was very little stress involved in his responsibilities. His duties were essentially to draw up finished construction drawings from engineering sketches, and he did it very well.

This is around the time when the Tommy/Marie betrayal occurred and he began to get a little paranoid about people. After all, the two closest people he had known, loved and trusted had deceived him. Would he ever be able to trust anyone again? Would he ever be able to get close to anyone again - male or female? The answer was no, at least not for a very long time. Shortly thereafter, he left Denver for what he believed were bigger and better opportunities. Even while in Denver he remembers going out to a nightclub once in two years. He had become a shut-in at the ripe old age of 24. Never going out for fear someone was out to "get him."

XII

A NEW DIRECTION

In March of 1977, Billy moved to San Francisco. After a couple of weeks of job hunting he found one with a small architectural/engineering firm. Design and Engineering Systems designed mostly industrial office parks. He never got to do any architectural design because he was working with designers from Berkeley and Harvard. His duties were primarily structural drafting but occasionally he got to work on some very interesting architectural designs. What he didn't know was that the place was a sweatshop. For months he was working 70 hours a week, then when things slowed down they simply let him go. But when things picked up again they called and asked him to come back. He told them no, of course, there was too much work out there to work for a company like that.

He quickly found another job with Kyle Apaydin - Architect. His office was in his home, which was in Oakland. Billy's apartment was in Foster City and the daily commute was about an hour long by car. He was only there a few months and he doesn't remember if Kyle let him go or if he moved on voluntarily. He does remember driving home some evenings screaming his lungs out in the car trying to release some of the stress built up during the day. He would get home in the evenings so stressed out he couldn't sleep nights. He'd go shoot baskets, go for a swim or a jog around the marina but nothing helped. At one time he went to a hypnotist but at a dollar a minute that was beyond his means even though he helped him to sleep one night.

Eventually, he went to work for the Bechtel Corporation. Their office was in downtown San Francisco and at the time employed nearly 9,000 people in several high-rise buildings. He interviewed with Rob Runnels who hired Billy because he was impressed with some of his own architectural creations. These "ideas" of his were drawings thought up during many sleepless nights (See Architectural Drawings). His valuable experience as a structural design/drafter didn't hurt either.

This company designed and constructed some of the biggest projects in the world. He briefly worked on the Waste Isolation Pilot Plant project in Carlsbad, New Mexico. He also worked briefly on the Saudi Arabia

International Airport, The Dubai International Airport and several other jobs. At one time he was given the responsibility of doing the conceptual design for a catering facility for the Dubai Airport Project. Bechtel was not awarded the bid for that job so he never got to see his design come to fruition.

XIII

ARCHITECTURAL DRAWINGS

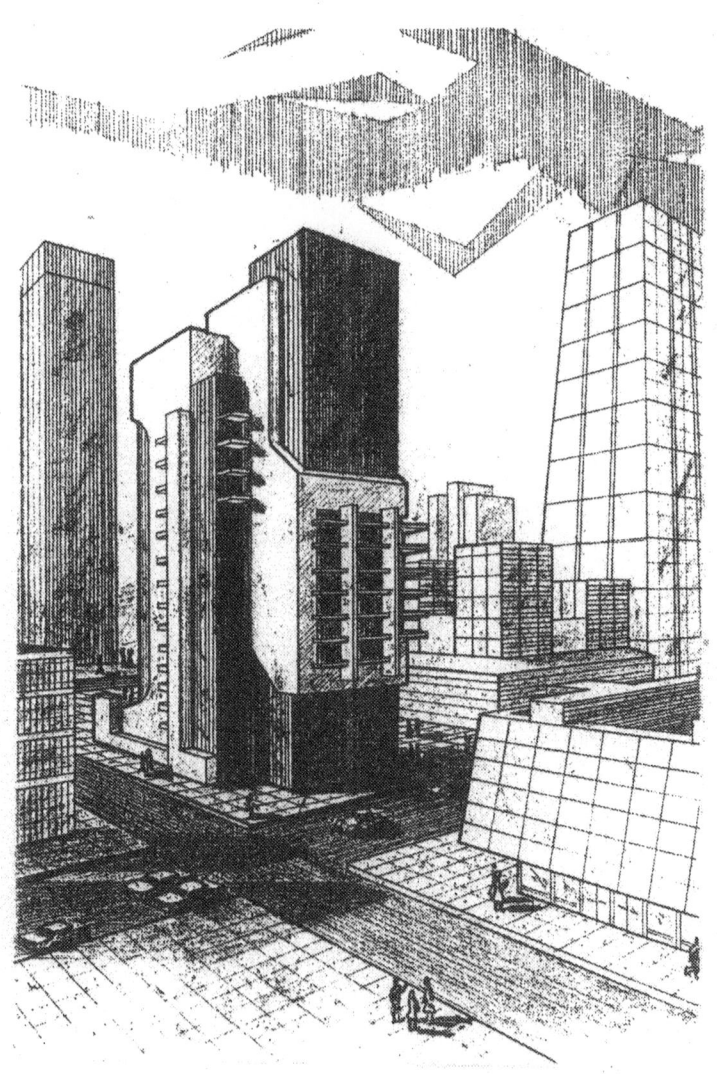

Study of a high-rise building

Study of high-rise towers with separate elevator shafts
The two towers and elevator shafts are connected with bridges

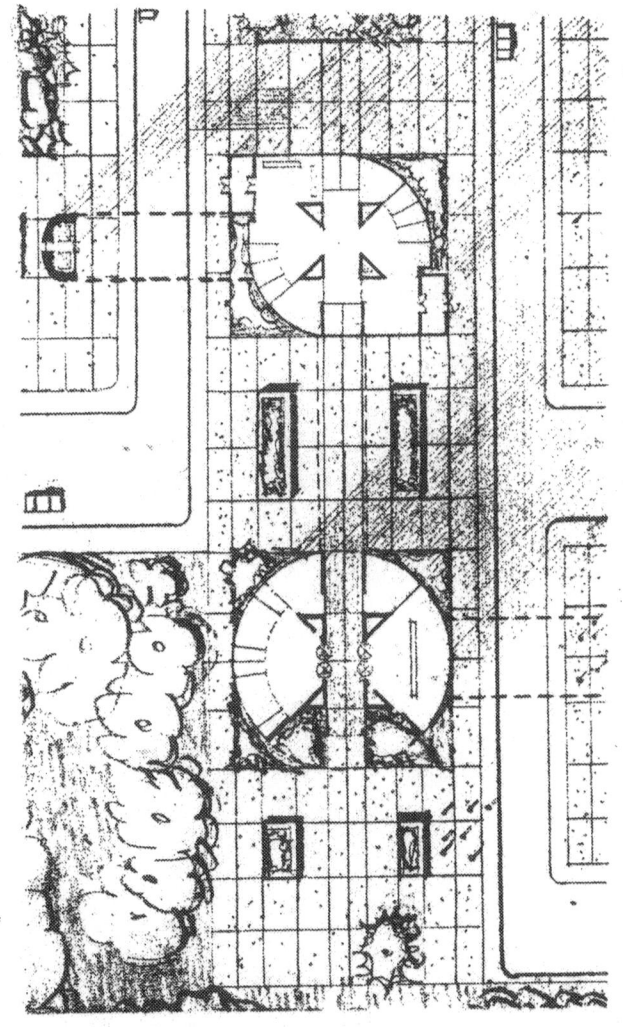

Ground Floor Plan of the Two Towers high-rise

Study of a city with densely populated downtown area showing many levels
of vehicular and pedestrian traffic. The levels of streets and walkways pass through and
are actually supported by the building's structure.

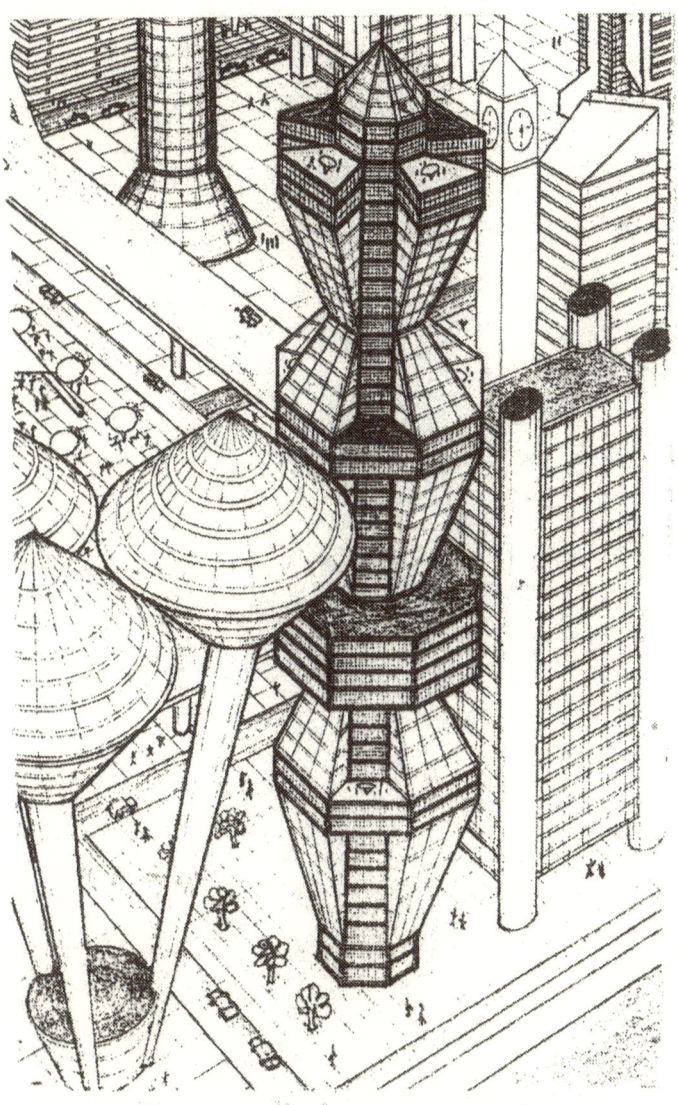

Study for a Highrise building with theme other
Than the conventional square or circle.

XIV

ESCAPE FROM SAN FRANCISCO

Billy's "escape" from the San Francisco Bay Area was done in such desperation it was almost comical. He left his apartment without notice. He dumped his furniture. Actually, he gave it to the janitor. What he couldn't fit into his little 1977 Toyota Celica he tossed into the dumpster. On the road he realized he was hungry because he probably hadn't eaten for days. But, every time he stopped to eat somewhere he wouldn't completely stop because he thought everyone was out to get him. He finally drove into McDonald's and bought a hamburger and a coke and paid with a $20 then left without his change because there were people in line behind him that he thought were talking about him. He thought they knew who he was and were trying to control his thoughts.

On the highway, every time he saw a police car he made a U turn because he thought they were looking for him. On the freeway he was deliberately hoping and even trying to get into an accident. At one time, he squeezed in between two 18-wheelers that were driving very close and very fast hoping they would run him over. All night he drove like a madman headed for his Aunt Sara's in Los Angeles.

While driving through San Luis Obispo he heard sirens blasting in the opposite direction. Fearing it was the police who had been waiting and were now coming for him, he took the nearest exit and hid somewhere in a darkened neighborhood. He stayed there until it was quiet, then threw the rest of his stuff into the nearest dumpster he could find. A car full of teenagers saw him and asked what the hell he was doing. He told them that if they wanted what he was throwing away that they could take it because he didn't need it. Suits, a guitar, a television, books and he didn't know what else he threw away.

When he finally got to Los Angeles he was thinking that if the police wanted him, they could have him. He drove straight into the police station and parked in their underground parking lot. From there he went to and sat on the steps of the police station expecting to be hauled away any minute. Nothing happened. He just sat there like an idiot in the middle of the night. Finally, he walked to the nearest payphone, which he found in the nearest bar, and called his aunt to come and get him. Somehow he had managed to end up only a few blocks away from where she lived so his aunt and uncle came and picked him up within 15 minutes. They went for his car and drove it to their house. All the while he was afraid that if the police saw his car they'd know where he was and they'd come get him. That night he heard helicopters flying overhead and woke his aunt up in desperation telling her, "There they are. They're looking for me. They're coming to get me." He couldn't sleep, he couldn't eat and he certainly couldn't think straight in his paranoid and schizophrenic state of mind. He didn't know what the hell was happening to him.

XV

<u>HOME AGAIN</u>

The next thing he remembers is being in an Albuquerque psychiatric ward in a straight jacket tied to a bed. After a few days in the hospital the good doctor gave him a prescription for Haldol and sent him home. All was fine again - his behavior was back to normal and he was thinking straight. Furthermore, UPS miraculously delivered all the "stuff" he had dumped in San Luis Obispo to his parents' home in Albuquerque.

After a few months of rest, good food and loving attention he felt well enough to go out looking for a job. The job he found was right up his alley - structural, civil and architectural drafting. There, he was settled in and secure for a few years and all the while thinking that his paranoid way of thinking was normal. He was always suspicious of his co-workers and was never able to trust anyone to get close to him physically, emotionally or socially.

XVI

DESPERATE   TIMES

Subsequently, there were other, more serious hospitalizations. Suicide attempts became routine - some of them were almost laughable.   In one instance, he was so isolated and feeling worthless that he tried to hang himself.   In his apartment, there was a TV cable cord coming out of the wall. He cut it about 6 feet long, put a plastic bag around his head, wrapped the cord around his neck, tied his hands and legs behind his back with a rope to his waist, climbed on a chair in the closet then kicked the chair out from under him with his knees. He hung there until the cord broke. His thinking was that if the cord broke he wouldn't be able to untie himself and would suffocate. Not so. He lay there for fifteen, maybe twenty minutes groping on the floor till he untied himself and got up. All he got for his effort was a temporary scar around his neck.

In the same apartment on the same night he tried cutting his wrist with a dull pocketknife. All he got out of that was a small scar on his left wrist and a ruined, blood-stained purple windbreaker. He wasn't finished yet though.

Next, he went to the nearest 24-hour pharmacy and bought two boxes of the Extra Strength Excedrin. On the way home he bought a large coke with ice, dissolved the pills in the coke and began to drink. He drank and drank until he consumed almost all his concoction. Wouldn't you know it, his Father came knocking at his door that morning and found him half asleep/half drugged and the evidence of his stupidity all over the bedroom.

Again, he was hospitalized. Again, he was diagnosed as a paranoid schizophrenic, given a prescription for a few weeks supply of anti-psychotics and sent home. In his then mental state there was just no way he could hold down any kind of a job. Especially considering that he was in denial that he was suffering from a serious mental illness. What to do? He couldn't hold a job, couldn't relate to people and couldn't think straight, so he joined the Army.

XVII

INTO THE MILITARY

He had been out of work for six months. He was unaware of how serious schizophrenia could become if not treated early. The Army seemed like the perfect solution to his problem. He filled out the questionnaire they gave him. Whatever his answers were, they were good enough to get him in.

In September of 1985, He was sent to Basic Training in Fort Jackson, South Carolina as an Administrative Specialist. Basic was not an easy duty. He went in at 208 pounds and came out at 183 and in great shape. Physically, he was able to complete all exercises except one (the 28 kilometer march) that was just too much for him. In spite of the fact that he went in as a 33 year old soldier and was competing with 18, 19 and 20 year old soldiers, he finished somewhere near the top of his class. He qualified Expert with the rifle. The other two soldiers his age were allowed to slide on practically every exercise except meals.

Advanced Individual Training (AIT) came next and it was fun for him. There were girls in the classes - lots of girls, ugly ones as well as pretty ones. He had two proposals of marriage before he got out of AIT. He didn't say no, he suggested they get to know each other first. They never did. They went their way and he went to Germany.

In Germany, he was stationed in a small detachment near the North Sea called Hohinkirchen. Their mission was to guard two underground nuclear bomb silos that he never saw. He was there 6 or 7 months, he didn't clearly remember, but he never went out to the "field." His job was to be an Administrative Assistant to the First Sergeant and the Commanding Officer. He typed out letter after letter after letter for them and did his very best to complete the task at hand without worrying about what others were doing. He co-operated with their mission to the extent of his responsibilities and no further. He woke up at 4:30 every morning to go to Physical Training (PT) at 5:30. He was at work every day from 7:30 am to 5:00pm. In other words he did his very best to be the best soldier he could possibly be for as long as he was physically and mentally able.

Sometime around September or October of 1986, his life began to spiral out of control. The paranoia, the delusions and the freight train he was hauling behind him started to run him over.   It all began when he was placed on his first 24-hour shift and he began to lose sleep.   The responsibilities he had were much more than just typing letters for the bosses. It meant staying up day and night observing and responding to correspondence between other detachments with their same mission. The stress reached an unmanageable level.   But this time it was acute stress.

XVIII

EUROPEAN VACATION

In an effort to relieve the stress Billy decided to take a vacation. With him in Germany, were his 3 young nephews and their mother (Freddie's widow) with whom he had at the time a loving relationship. They all climbed into his green 1977 BMW and started to tour Europe. They went west from West Germany to Holland then southwest to Belgium and further south to Paris, France.

They spent the first night either in Amsterdam or Brussels and the next two or three nights in Paris at the Phenix Hotel near the Arc de Triomphe in downtown Paris. The second night in Paris, Myra and he went to the Moulin Rouge and it was great for them. The next day they were back on the road for another 8 or 9 hours. He wasn't relieving any stress - just making his condition worse.

Nevertheless, they continued with plans to drive into Madrid, Spain. By the time they got to Spain he could understand the radio stations disc jockeys and it seemed to him as if they were all talking about him. It seemed as if they knew his every move. Every time he stopped for gas he could swear all those people knew who he was and that they were trying to control his every thought. Needless to say, they didn't make it to Madrid - instead, they stopped in Zaragoza. They went there because he somehow knew the U. S. had an airbase there and they could stay and rest up for a couple of days. He was the only one needing the rest because they were all having a blast while he was dealing with a torrential rain inside his brain.

They rested and he dealt with the situation as best he could, then headed back to Germany. On the way back they went through Barcelona and he had enough awareness in him to find a couple of Antonio Gaudi's architectural masterpieces. One he clearly remembers visiting is the Sagrada Familia Cathedral. They had lunch outside across the street on the sidewalk. Afterwards, they headed straight back to Paris for a couple more days of rest then back to Germany.

He returned to work no more rested than before. In fact, he was worse. He was already unable to sleep and think rationally when a phone call came from home with news that his father had had an aneurysm and was critically ill. He immediately drove to Munich with Charles (his nephew) to catch a flight to Albuquerque. When they arrived his father was in a coma at the VA hospital. They were in Albuquerque for a few days and when it seemed he might recover they returned to Germany.

He was back in Germany only a few days when his sister, Ruth, called to inform him that their father had died. Once again he drove to Munich for a flight home with Nick (his other nephew). This time, on the way to Munich his suicidal thoughts were creeping in again and on a two-way highway construction zone he had it in his mind to end everything by just swaying the car ever so slightly to the left. Fortunately, he didn't go through with it. He and Nick arrived in Albuquerque safe and sound. Well, Nick was safe, but he was not sound, by any means.

He was so distraught, confused and paranoid that he didn't make it to his own father's funeral. Which was no surprise, since, he had a way of inadvertently avoiding funerals, particularly his own. Not only did he not make it to his father's funeral he didn't make it back to Germany. A couple of days after the funeral Nick and Billy caught a flight back through Dallas and that's as far as they got. He swears he heard his name again and again over the intercom system at the airport. He swears the announcer was saying, "There goes Billy, look at that idiot, don't let him get away, there he goes… Billy, where do you think your going? Billy, I'm talking to you… yea, you, Billy - you idiot… etc." He made a U turn inside the Dallas airport with Nick in hand and they headed straight back to Albuquerque. There, they spent 3 or 4 weeks until he thought it was "safe" to return to Germany. Eventually they made it back safely.

XIX

REALITY SINKS IN

Back on duty Billy was scheduled for his 24-hour shift which he completed successfully. But, on the way home he fell asleep behind the wheel and drove his car into a steel garage door knocking out a few teeth and briefly knocking himself out as well. Thereafter, he was grounded to the barracks day and night. He tried to explain to the Sergeant in command what was happening to him but he wouldn't listen.

It was his sister-in-law that drove him to the base hospital in Bremerhaven. The psychiatrist there immediately medicated him and made arrangements for him to be further evaluated in Mannheim. From there, he was medically evacuated to the States. The diagnosis by the Medical Evaluation Board at Sheppard Air Force Base in Wichita Falls was as follows: "schizoaffective disorder;

chronic, with recent acute exacerbation; severe, currently in remission on medication."

He now had no doubts about his mental health. He was schizophrenic and it was a chronic condition. The army gave him a few months supply of medication, released him from the hospital and discharged him with a good behavior medal. The Army said he should "receive psychiatric follow-up at a clinic of his choice". He was discharged in July of 1987.

Luckily, he located a clinic near his mother's house in Albuquerque and did receive the follow-up treatment. However, he was determined not to let this mental illness get the best of him. Shortly after his discharge, an engineering company hired him as a structural draftsman. He didn't last two months. The voices he heard in his brain and voices he heard outside of his brain wouldn't let him concentrate on the simplest tasks.

He was unable to work, and at his sister Laura's suggestion he applied for Social Security Disability. The first two applications were denied. How could they deny him with his medical track record? The judge, on the third appeal, approved his request for disability and in December of 1989, he began receiving a monthly check. It wasn't much, but it sure was a Godsend.

All was well for the next few years. A county program was providing him with the necessary medication and psychiatric treatment. Things were so good for his mother and him that they moved to the Heights in 1992. In 1994, he began having problems getting medication. Anti-psychotics are very expensive and Medicare will not cover them. The county program he was dependent on for his medication lost it's funding so he was without medication. Eventually, he became sick and suicidal and ended up in the hospital once again.

Following his discharge from the hospital he relied on sample medications from various doctors. He was put on Haldol, then Prolixin, then Thioridizine and eventually on Zyprexa. Between 1994 and 2004, he had a steady supply of medications and during that time never had any psychiatric problems. He was doing so well at one point that he went out and found a part time job. He started working in 1996, and continues to this day on a part-time basis.

XX

A SCHIZOPHRENIC EPISODE

As of December 24, 2003, his regular psychiatrist stopped giving him prescriptions and samples of Zyprexa, but he still had many, many samples and continued taking it until he discovered that it caused his diabetes. He learned about Zyprexa while watching television on the morning of April 2, 2004. He saw an ad for a law firm concerning the side effects caused by Zyprexa - diabetes was mentioned as one of its many side effects. Billy had been diagnosed with diabetes in April of 2001. Aware of the serious medical problems associated with diabetes, he was already fearful about it and was always cautious and deliberate about taking his medication for diabetes and followed a strict diabetic diet. Believing that the bad effects were worse than its anti-psychotic benefits, he immediately stopped taking Zyprexa.

As previously mentioned, Billy had no problems while he was on medication. However, in 2004, his 10-year streak without a schizophrenic episode came to an end. His psychiatrist informed him that he was going to semi-retire and he would have to find another psychiatrist to treat his schizophrenia.

After many phone calls he was finally able to find another psychiatrist to treat him and made a first appointment for April 14, 2004. He prescribed a daily dose of 10-15 mg of Abilify (Aripriprazole). For whatever reason, Abilify did not work for him and he soon began experiencing another schizophrenic episode. He was feeling very paranoid, worthless, guilty, and believed people were out to get him.

He took messages from the radio and TV personally. While watching TV at noon Wednesday, June 16, 2004, the weather lady gestured with her thumb (as if to hitch hike) and said, "Go to Tucumcari because the weather there is perfect." He felt as if she were talking directly to him so he went out the door and slowly began walking to Tucumcari.

He walked in the blistering heat through his neighborhood to King Road for about 10 miles and at one point picked up a discarded bottle of red Power Ade he found along the way and drank it to relieve his thirst. His immediate plan was to make it to a nearby water tank and spend the night there and continue in the morning.

Back home his mother looked for him but could not find him in the house, at friends' homes or anywhere in the neighborhood. She knew he had not been feeling well for several days and began to worry, but thought that maybe he had gone somewhere in the car so she looked in the garage and saw that both cars were still parked there. She also found his wallet with his ID and money on the nightstand in his room and then knew that something was not right. She called his sister Ruth in Las Cruces and told her he was missing. They immediately called the Heights Department of Public Safety and they put out a local APB for him. The Heights Police Department found him at about 7:00 that evening on King Road. With their sirens blasting, 3 or 4 patrol cars approached him and the police promptly told him to spread-eagle on the hood of one of the their cars. They frisked him, handcuffed him, and held him at gunpoint. They sat his butt on the side of the road and with a gun pointed at his head asked him if he knew what time it was and he said about 3:00. Then the gung-ho policewoman with the gun in her hand yelled out its 7:00. Once the police realized he was not a threat to himself or to others, they removed the handcuffs and placed him in the back of an ambulance. On the way to the hospital he told the paramedic that after the doctor examines him and finds him to be all right he would continue on his way to Tucumcari.

While in the exam room he was still very fearful of others and would not allow the nurse to put an IV in him because he thought they were going to poison him. It took 3 sisters 2 nurses and about 40 minutes to convince him that he was dehydrated and that he needed the IV for fluids. Blood was eventually drawn from him. After the blood test the doctor had reason enough to keep him overnight.

That night he was unable to eat, drink, or sleep and the following day, dressed in his hospital clothing, he attempted to leave the hospital through a nearby emergency exit. He managed to set off the alarm before his sister, her husband and a male nurse physically restrained him and convinced him to wait for the psychiatrist to examine him. Later the psychiatrist examined him and determined that he was not in complete control of his senses so he transferred him to the psychiatric ward. It had been over 10 years since he had been in that hospital so he knew what to expect in the mental ward. He was released the following Friday.

If he had made it to the water tank that day, and he was about 45 minutes away, there is no telling what would have happened to him. During his hike he decided not to go the long way around the bend to the water tank and took a short cut through the desert itself. He walked a mile or two through the sand and the bushes scaring a few jackrabbits and at one point heard a sudden crackling noise that scared the hell out of him. He had disturbed a live and clicking rattlesnake. When he realized he had almost stepped on a snake he decided to rest under the shade of a nearby pinon tree. After all, the threat from the dirt, the weeds, the stickers, the ants and the strange insects was no threat at all compared to a rattlesnake. While under the cool shade of the tree he took off his shoes, popped a few blisters and continued on his trek through the desert hoping to reach the water tank before dark. His plan was to spend the night on the side of the tank opposite the road where no one could see or find him. The next morning he was going to walk to Highway 550 (about 2 miles) and from there, another 2 miles to I-25 north through Santa Fe toward Denver completely unaware that Tucumcari was on east I-40.

During his hospital stay, his doctor advised him to reapply to the Veterans Administration for benefits. The doctor's immediate concern, however, was to find another source to provide medication. He was referred to Pathways, Inc., an agency that provides temporary psychiatric follow-up and samples of medication to patients in need. And, that's exactly what they did for him. He was a patient at Pathways for over a year. The attending psychiatrist there observed him closely and became aware of his complete medical history. With his help in providing the VA with the 'new evidence' they required he was awarded service-connected benefits. Finally, he had a permanent and reliable source of follow-up and medication.

XXI

<u>18 YEARS LOST</u>

The lack of accessibility to expensive anti-psychotics is not the only reason Billy has nearly lost his sanity and his life. He recently experienced an extremely stressful situation where he examined his own soundness of mind.

He and his mother had lived together for over 18 years. Following his military discharge in July of 1987, and until February of 2006, they lived under the same roof. They were both on Social Security - retirement pension and SSDI, respectively. They were both happy with their living arrangement and never bothered anyone for anything.

In November of 2004, He met a girl from Mexico, fell in love and decided to marry her and planned to bring her to New Mexico to live with him and his mother. When he disclosed his plans at a family meeting all hell broke loose. His sister, Janice, who had authority to make decisions for his mother under a General Durable Power of Attorney advised him that, "That'll never happen." At previous family meetings Janice had mentioned that 5 of his 7 sisters planned to place their mother in a nursing home. She was suffering from dementia and in the early stages of Alzheimer's disease. In previous family meetings the votes had all gone against him to keep their mother at home. Debra, Ruth, TJ and Billy wanted to keep her where she was but they were out numbered. Laura, Brenda, Janice, Angela and Teri voted to send her away. In the end, it didn't really matter what the votes were because Janice was determined to put her out to pasture.

XXII

POWER OF ATTORNEY

Ironically, it was Billy's doing that gave Janice the POA. In 1995, he suggested to his mother that she have a Will drafted and he assisted her in finding a lawyer to do just that. He also suggested their mother appoint Janice as executor of the Will because, at that time, she was well in control of her life situation. Laura and his mother never really got along; Brenda lived in El Paso; Debra lived in Mississippi; Billy was unstable; Ruth lived in Houston; and Angela, TJ and Teri had young families they were raising. It was fitting - he thought Janice able to make wise decisions. After all, she was a schoolteacher in control of a classroom. Unknowingly, the lawyer tossed in a POA with the Will and listed Janice as their mother's Power of Attorney.

Ruth, Billy and Debra went to court in an attempt to keep her out of a nursing home, or at least the place they wanted to send her - Manzano Springs. She would have been placed in lock-down - a memory-loss unit with approximately 29 other Alzheimer's elderly "inmates." Some were trying to escape, others walking around with soiled undergarments, and most looking generally very unhappy. Imagine what a madhouse that would have been for their mother. But, as the oldest sister, Laura, put in the last family meeting "we're not thinking of her we're thinking of us" (referring to Laura, Brenda, Janice, Angela, Teri). That is exactly what they were thinking. This they knew because Janice had already made a deposit at Manzano Springs, and the marketing director called his mother's number to ask if Janice was still placing her mother there. Coincidentally, Ruth answered the phone and was mistaken by the director to be Janice.

For Billy, personally, this was horrible. Imagine living with someone you love for 18 years - him looking after her and her looking after him as much. They were a team for nearly two decades that was broken up late in the last quarter. She is currently living in a place where she doesn't want to be. Every time he visits her she tells him she won't be there tomorrow. She wants him to "call before he goes to visit her there because she has to go to her work at her mother's house." According to her, it was her father that built the house she is in now and all the houses in that neighborhood, and she has to work in her house in Albuquerque. She is well looked after in that home but why should she be living with strangers when she can be with someone that is family and who genuinely loves her. As it is now, he is "allowed" under the POA's rules, to see her only 1½ hours a week 3 times a month. How much more thoughtless can someone be?

Before the Alzheimer's, some of his sisters visited his mother only 4, maybe 5 times a year if they were in the area. Maybe they'd bring her flowers on Easter or Mother's Day, buy her a gift on Christmas, occasionally throw her a birthday party. What did he do? He'd check her doors and windows every night; and drive her places like California, Texas, Arizona and Oklahoma. And, who knows how many times he drove her to Grants to visit relatives, not to mention a trip to Puerto Rico and Orlando. For years he cooked breakfast, lunch and dinner for her. He took her to the doctor many, many times. He'd take her out to eat, even it was just fast food, and to church when she was still able to go. And what did that get him - a letter in the mail, telling him he can see her 3 times next month.

How was he able to deal with his schizophrenia during this horrendous experience? The stress was worse than what he had experienced while in the military, in California, in Colorado or anywhere else. He had suicidal thoughts creeping in his brain, but that would have been cowardly especially when he thought about what that would have done to his mother. There were times when he felt like striking out physically at someone - but who? Sometimes he thought about going to a bar and starting a fight but that might have gotten him killed in a most unsightly way. He thought about throwing a chair through a window in some business establishment - but that would have landed him in a straight jacket. He thought about crashing his car, overdosing on his meds, this and that. He finally said to himself "Hang in there - it will be over soon." And it was - but not quite the way he wanted. Yes, his Mother is taken care of but she does not want to be there!

What is going to happen when she can no longer be where she is? Once she becomes a "two-person lift" she will no longer be welcomed there. Once she runs out of money she will no longer be welcomed there. Which ever comes first - and one of those two scenarios will take place before her demise.

As for Billy and his family, well, all things considered, they serve the Lord first and believe because of it are rich in happiness and in many other ways as well. His struggle with schizophrenia is by no means over. He deals with paranoia, anxiety and feelings of guilt everyday. Not to mention the occasional voices inside his mind, thoughts of suicide, messages from the radio and television that disrupt his thinking, isolation, and the inability to relate to people that he has to fight off everyday. His condition, the experts say, is caused by a chemical imbalance inside his brain. However, as long as he has a reliable supply of medication, follow-up treatment and stable life without undo stress, he can and will overcome this affliction he lives with.

XXIII

<u>DREAMS</u>

The following is a collection of dreams that Billy recorded from night to night. They are included because they might be of interest since some of them are so strange and allegorical compared to the dreams of people without schizophrenia. They often take him back to his hometown of Grants and the places in his childhood like familiar fields he used to run through but in his dreams he gets lost in them. The University of New Mexico campus is a frequent location of his dreams - another place where he gets lost. Many childhood friends he knew in Grants frequently appear. Of course, his immediate family members and people who have significant meaning at this time in his life also frequently appear together in incomprehensible situations. Three common themes that occur often in his dreams are running, fighting and getting lost.

3/20/06

I had a nightmare that Mom and I were in Cloudcroft, New Mexico driving around in her 2001 Ford Escort. There was a tremendous flood that flooded the car so we had to get out and walk. I tried to get help but no one would help. I went into a restaurant and asked 2 ladies to help and they said no. We walked around till she got too weak so I carried her. Then we got lost, couldn't find her yellow Cutlass Ciera car. So tired were we that we had to lie down on the side of a hill. Then, three bullies came and started fighting with me. I flagged down a trucker who came and helped. Mom was also behind me throwing jabs at the bullies. Then I woke up

- I have had this dream before once or twice in the past
- In the dream I remembered punching but my punches had no power

3/21/06

I dreamed that Lena and I were doing it at that little hotel (La Hacienda in Janos, Mexico) outside on the second floor - then people started coming out of the woods little by little till a lot of people were around us. I ended up in her pants and she in mine.

3/24/06

I dreamed I was picking up beads from the floor to make jewelry. I saw two brown triangular shaped earrings with three silver stripes on each side of the earrings.

On the same night I dreamed I was at a gate where there were 2 guards in green jump suits. At the gate people were trying to get past the gate but couldn't at first but then eventually forced themselves through.

3/28/06

I dreamed of a University that changes its purpose and name every semester. There are 4 semesters per year.
    1 University of Physics
    2 University of Golf
    3 University of Academics
    4 University of something else
A university where students leave the school with money, and it takes 16 semesters to graduate and students pick which subjects the school teaches each semester. Students pick the 16 most important subjects to be taught by the university. Theo of the Bill Cosby Show was the person explaining to me how their university worked.

3/29/06

I had a dream that two young African American boys were throwing darts at me. I asked them, "What does that get you?" Their mother walked in and they were trying to explain to her what they were doing. Then I woke up...

3/30/06

I dreamed there was a great big red infection on the apex of my right bicep muscle. I started looking for my shoes to go to the VA hospital. Then the red infection went down but I could see live tiny little bugs moving around under my skin in my arm. Janice told me where my shoes were. I went outside looking for my car and there were cars all around our little green house on Highway 66 in Grants but I couldn't find my car there. I saw TJ's yellow VW and was going inside to get my keys to go to the VA but my feet wouldn't move fast enough then I went to his car but the door handle was broken so I went to another car and was taking a leak.

- there was a woman with a red rifle in the dream also
- and a red truck driving to the backyard also in the dream

4/1/06

I dreamed 2 pit bulls were trying to get me.

4/2/06

Dreamed I was on a cruise ship eating and eating and eating till there was no food or places to sit. I had to stand and got stuck with a complete blue fish.

4/3/06

I dreamed I was in the army and a soldier handed me an envelope with 3 large wedding gold bands linked together.

4/6/06

I Dreamed I went on a trip in a bus, forgot my luggage but got on anyway - sat in the first seat to the left. Seats were black and dusty - we were being led through some very rough roads by a truck and man on a horse. At one time I saw a yellow dog and a spotted dog chasing each other. I gave a quarter to a little boy - a man in the back was talking but I don't remember what he was saying except that he said, "He's already talked to the boy."

4/7/06

I dreamed I was going on a trip. I had to stand in line to get permission to go. Coach Wallace (from Junior and High School) was the agent-in-charge and when it was my turn to get my tickets he wanted me to eat snails. I wouldn't and told him his trip was a waist of time and money and I would rather not go. (I was going to Ireland or Denmark). Some girl took the snail with the coach and they both put it in their mouth together as in a kiss, but this still didn't convince me to eat the snail. A little boy in cowboy gear (boots, chaps, hat, etc) said he would eat them and he got up from the table at which he was sitting and ate the snail and took a drink of coke to swallow it down - only to turn around and vomit or spit it out then I clapped… But he didn't spit up the snail he spit up a crab into the floor. Then I woke up

- I was different because I was an expert with a rifle so they had to search me
- There were people all around watching and waiting for me to eat the snail - but I would not

4/8/06

Dreamed I was checking the air in the three car's tires. I backed up my car and got stuck in the sand. We're going on a one-day trip I told mom and she said, "Yes, I packed for one day."

- Also dreamed I was playing basketball outdoors on a goal like the one I had in Grants. I hit a couple of baskets but then couldn't buy a basket.
- Also dreamed I was at a big party walking around looking for the boss "to settle a scam." I went from room to room - there were people everywhere.
- Finally, a foreign girl asked me where she could get a milkshake - I picked her and her friend up and went in my yellow car to get a milkshake.

4/10/06

Dreamed I was at a practice watching Kansas' football team offense run through drills. It was hailing slightly and I didn't have a jacket. I was asked what time it was by someone sitting on the fence. It was 7:30. I told him - Utah was picked even by the Mountain West Conference and Kansas was picked by 6 by their conference. I ran home, crossed a bridge, and climbed a little hill. Irma (a Mexican lady who cared for my mother for a while) was waiting to give me a hand but I climbed it alone just fine... Went in the house and looked in the refrigerator. It was almost empty - walked around the house and my father was taking care of a young kid. Freddie was running a restaurant next door. A.J. and TJ had signed for some plastic trays and I told them to send them back. There was a real, real tall African-American that was part of the family with a briefcase in his hand and he sat on a desk and laughed.

- (the run was a familiar path I used to take when I was young - from Mesa Vista Elementary across the field to cross 66 home)
- I also dreamed he, Greg and Ruth were in an old Ford station-wagon convertible parked near a wall - we were all going to sleep in the car because it was late and dark.

Ruth woke up scared because there was a lamp that woke her up - I told her I bumped my head. Then, I realized there was a man on top of her and I started to scream cause I couldn't move - the man fled over Greg. I and another man started to come back - I was actually grunting and grunting but couldn't move then woke up realizing it was a dream.

4/11/06

Had a dream that Debra told me - "Laura sold the muds." I told her "You can turn her in for that"

4/13/06

Dreamed I was visiting mom behind bars and I knew how to break the combination of the safe to let mom out of her cell - the only problem was it was physically hurting her. The ladies there agreed she did not belong there. She could still be the first lady if she wanted to. There was someone behind her helping work the numbers of the safe.

4/14/06

Dreamed I had my corvette with 3 or 4 people inside wanting to go for a ride. Also dreamed I was on a bike with 2 people behind me going through backyards till I got on the highway.

4/15/06

I had a dream about Coach Bowlls - he called me a pretender. The dream was when I was a junior in high school.

4/19/06

I had a vision in my dream of me having dinner at a table and Teri was there with many people there. The people wanted to hurt me somehow but I got in a 4 x 4 that belonged to Teri. It was parked on a cliff and I started to go backwards and then tried to stop it by using the brakes but finally let it go backwards and drove it till I got control and was driving away from everyone. Then there were many people and a bright light in the sky - Jesus is coming in a spaceship, a beautiful, beautiful gold and silver spaceship. The light was so bright it was blinding and there were many, many people. Jesus started to look for me. Finally, Jesus went down in the crowd in his spaceship till he found me. Jesus started to question me for my past behavior, which was never good. He asked me questions and I answered with biblical answers. It ended up that he gave me 1000 years because it is written in the bible.

- He was speaking in a wonderfully loud voice
- He had a large entourage following him
- At one time there was only gibberish coming out of my mouth
- He threatened to drown me in the ocean for ever and ever
- But I asked for 1000 more years
- If I didn't straighten up in 1000 years He would burn me in hell for ever
- And all my family with me
- My family was some kind of royal family

Jesus named a lot of girls that couldn't have babies because of me and one committed suicide

- But she was welcomed in heaven

4/21/06

Dreamed I had a chance to play basketball with the Greek All Stars - They were practicing in my backyard in Grants.

4/24/06

Dreamed I ran into Cecil Quiroja, Barbara Woolworth and Jimmy Mendez at UNM. Cecil was asking Jimmy for money but I lost them in the campus crowd. Also dreamed that someone in a big black limousine was looking for a notary - I told them to follow me but they drove off - I went looking for Brenda because she was a notary but got lost in the UNM campus crowd.

4/29/06

I dreamed I was walking on water on special steel shoes around the house because there was an SUV looking for me.

- I had special steel shoes that allowed me to walk on water

4/30/06

I dreamed I was going in the Library downtown but they didn't let me in because there was a fire so I walked down the stairs to the lower level on very steep stairs. When I got down there I was in a wheel chair and a girl who also was in a wheel chair came to talk to me. She showed me some very beautiful jewelry she had made. She was in a class and when her teacher came she got up and walked away but I couldn't walk away because I couldn't walk.

- I also put my wheel chair down some kind of incinerator then went looking for it.

5/5/06

I dreamed Ruth had hooked me up with 4 business people from the office of Financial Management in Santa Fe and I was supposed to make a lot of money for my family.

- She hooked me up with a Mr. Gutierrez and 3 other business ladies with names too difficult to pronounce
- I was also outside picking up nails and putting them in a bucket with water

5/6/06

I dreamed Bobby Haffway was trying to take my home away and was fighting him and his ex-con friends off with chairs and guns then finally got police help.

5/8/06

I dreamed Greg wasn't going to fix my car till Friday

- Freddie answered the door and Alice came in with a message
- Brenda walked in the door with a wedding dress on and Freddie said, "Modernists"

Greg and Brenda were going to get married - I went to put my suit on but couldn't because Alice when she was small kept coming in the room and wouldn't let me change my underwear. I finally had to carry her to the door and put an ironing board on the door for her to stay out. I told A.J., "Don't let her in."

5/21/06

Had a dream that I saw Kenny Cotton at my 20th reunion in High School and in my dream I was in High School at the time. Someone came up to me and said that's because you are 50 years old and I said well "What am I doing here?" Kenny and another man started talking about explosives they had used in Viet Nam.

5/29/06

Had a dream that me, Jerry and James Manning were running through school campus. Some teacher accused me of stealing a blue plastic paper holder. I said it wasn't me it was Clyde - as Jerry was caught in the act.

5/31/06

I dreamed that Lena was with another man - another man in a blue shirt.

6/6/06

Dreamed I was walking down a long church hallway with big windows on the right and a man big as an elephant was coming my way. There wasn't enough room for both of us so I jumped out the window and there was a big dog outside. I jumped out on a ledge the dog kept jumping too. Then I ran into Jerry Alberts, he wasn't very friendly.

6/10/06

Dreamed my Uncle Frank had an 18-wheeler and I stole it and was using it to drive on the weekend. It was a huge black truck. I parked it in a Houston 18-wheeler parking lot but got lost trying to go to it. I was going up and down stairs and in and out of hallways and bumped into Francie Garcia and her boyfriend who were also truckers. They asked me if I had gone to the party. I said. "No, I was on the road." Trying to get to my truck I ran into Candy Peterson. Another girl was trying to help me get to my truck. I saw it from a distance but couldn't get to it. The girl told me to go down this chute but I couldn't fit. I said "Let's go another way - there was some kind of gathering of Truckers because the President was in the area." That's why I couldn't get to my truck. They were checking ID's and I didn't have a trucker's ID so I avoided that line. A police stopped me and asked me what I was doing going down that chute - I told him I was lost. He let me go but I couldn't get to his truck then I woke up.

6/11/06

I had a dream they took Lena to a Chinese High-rise building and made her a prostitute. I went in the building with C2 explosives and blew the place up. They were arresting everyone outside and putting them in a line then photographing them then putting them into jail. I saw Lena in a group photo dressed as a geisha girl with white face. I went to her but it wasn't her - I smeared her face with my hand then Remy Busick came up and stopped me from behind and said, "You should quit." She was on drugs.

6/12/06

I had a dream I was playing tennis with Robert. He was hitting the balls way up to me. Then, I was hitting them down to him.

7/7/06

On a day when I get no mail   I had a dream about getting tons of Christmas cards.

7/28/06

I had a dream about a golf club that would hit the ball 500 yards

7/29/06

Had a dream about Silvey Rodriguez and everybody was wearing sweaters and had another dream about teaching a little boy how to use a flat shovel.

8/8/06

I dreamed that 4 or 5 bullies were pushing me around. One asked me if he understood English. They were physically shoving me around but I was shoving right back. Then I told the one on the right, you speak Beach. That psyched him out. Then I told the other 2 in the middle leave me alone because I'll psyche you out like I did your friend. The two looked at their friend and saw how he was spaced out. That stunned them too then they quit bullying him. The one on the left followed me to my car then he went away also. I was in a hospital then, sat in a chair and a nurse came to me to put a stethoscope on my left hand and I told her to leave me alone, I came to see my child.

8/9/06

Dreamt another guy and me broke into a school we tossed around files and books then got caught. While there, another short guy joined us and we broke into a room that was full of pennies, we ran away got on a bus. I had $25.00 it cost me $13.50 for a ticket. One guy sat on the step of the door, the other guy sat on a seat and I sat on a fat ladys' lap for a while then I was too heavy, got up sat in her wheel chair while she sat on someone's lap then she wrapped her legs around me. One guy said he doesn't hear the sirens. Then the driver knows what we were doing and made a U turn to avoid the cops chasing us.

- I didn't know it myself but the short guy had shot someone with his left hand and that's why the cops were after us.

8/11/06

Dreamt there was a big spotted dog in the backyard. I shooed him away at first then he came back then there were other dogs, big black dogs that wouldn't leave. I tried spraying them with Raid and other stuff, whatever I could find but the dog was so big he came at me. Then, I saw A.J. on the other side of the dogs but he couldn't walk though he was taking steps. He wouldn't get any closer. I yelled out to him "Get in here A.J." but the dogs were not attacking him, then I woke up.

8/12/06

I dreamt of the apocalypse - the same thing that happened in Indonesia happening here. Floods, buildings coming down on people, water swallowing up everything, having to get up on the highest ground possible. A friend of mine was trying to climb a building that was falling down, seeing one side of the building fall on a couple of ladies. Then running to higher ground on top of a small building then the owner grabbing me from behind trying to save his home but my friend helped me. My friend climbed in the window and out with a big stick to hit the owner with it to get him off me. Then a big jeep was almost running me off the top of the hill. There was a boy with a gun, which I took away from him then 2 girls came up to me because we had the gun.

8/26/06

Dreamed I was in a fight with some guy, a real knock down drag out fight. We were shoving each other first then throwing rocks at each other, then punching each other then I got a gun and woke up.

8/29/06

Dreamed mom had all the appliances upside down in the kitchen and was putting new wheels on them. Especially bad were the refrigerator wheels.

I dreamed that I was in a recliner that could be driven like a car. I turned the key and took off on the city streets like a car.

8/31/06

I had the most wonderful dream that I was ice-skating with Ellie Burton (a grade school sweetheart). Then, TJ insulted her and she put a headband on like an Indian. She said that I had kicked a pig and I said, "You remembered that." We went up a little room then back down some very steep stairs while holding hands. She wanted me to kiss her but I was married. While putting the skates on I had some trouble with the shoe strings because some of the clips were broken so I just tied the strings around my leg.

XXIV

SOME PASSING THOUGHTS

Also included, are random, troubling thoughts Billy recorded one night because they were keeping him awake.

What purpose is there in life? Why do I breathe and eat and sleep and talk and walk? I am married but I'm still alone. I am loved by my family, friends, neighbors and co-workers, (I think), but I'm still alone. At times I sleep with someone but usually I sleep alone. I work, I play, and come and go when need be. I do what is right in the eyes of man and hopefully in God's eyes too. But what does it get me - I am still by myself.

When I stumble I ask to be forgiven. I pray… a little. I pray a lot. I work hard at times and not so hard some other times. But I always go to work - even though it's menial labor… It's honest, it pays lousy, but it pays the bills and keeps me afloat from day to day.

God loves me, I'm told. Jesus loves me too. I've heard it said in song, in rhyme from preachers and strangers alike.

What purpose is there in waking up tomorrow - to see the sunrise; to see another day; to see my stepdaughter; to see my wife; to be with myself again?

And when I sleep - I dream stuff incomprehensible to me. Why sleep? What meaning is there in my dreams? What meaning is there in life? What purpose do I have in this life? To eat, drink and be merry? Nope certainly not that, but yes sometimes just that. I get up on my roof so it won't leak. I cut the grass so it looks good. I pull weeds. I fix the plumbing. I fix what needs to be fixed - but for what purpose? What reason do I have to live if at the beginning of the day and the middle of the day and the end of the day I'm alone. The depth of solitude I feel at times is as vast and deep and dark as the empty night skies. How do I fill it with purpose with meaning with reason with something? How do I fill it with something? Fill it with hope? Hope for what? What do I hope for? Hope I make it to heaven. Hope I don't make it to hell. Hope I'm not alone tomorrow when I'm alone right now.

Jesus says "I am the way the truth the life, no one goes to the father but by me" And in the meantime I'm alone. Is that my cross?

XXV

POEMS

The reason these few poems are included is because Billy likes to write poetry and thought it might be helpful and interesting to read his poems. Some of these poems rhyme, some don't. Some of them make sense and some don't. Hopefully, they will all be interesting to peruse.

UNTITLED POEM

Vernacular - brown and
Semi-arid - tundra, trees, tamarisk and
Tumbleweeds   Plateau, malpais, mountains
Snow, snow, snow at
Least 28 below. Heat
Wind   dust, dust, dust   torrent rain
Sudden flood, calm creek flow fast
Dry arroyo flood wet

I'm happy - condition complete - Contentment
Peaceful as a Sunday song
Listen…   to a birdsong
A sparrow or whippoorwill
I cannot see, such beauty fades

Under thunder sky
And smoke screened eye
Fortitude, social fortitude
Impetus too strong
But the darkness around me, beyond me is far.
Night abides in me in
Deed, the motions I make, the words
I say - Incomprehensible glitters
Of light searching, searching, searching
For fuse. Incapacitated glimmers of
Pride.   Cannot this self as it is
Strengthen this system
This person within
All those tales that I read
All those times that I've flown

All those prophets I heard
All those poems poorly written
All those days without God - taken
Along with a tongue that's become shallow
All those words not worth the mention
Along with you and me - soon forgotten.

ADAM'S REPRIEVE

What more is there to conceive
Of the fate of Adam and Eve?

What wrath have they wrought?
Unto them God said "Thou shalt not."

But the serpent did beguile Eve
Then Adam did she deceive.

With all her cunning means
Wrenched his peaceful dreams.

God created Adam in his likeness
Knowing Eve would surely like this.

Of all the creatures God did make
She alone could Adam's manhood wake.

God did say: Live ye in the Garden of Eden
But take ye not of the fruit forbidden.

But the serpent (repulsive and vile)
Did tempt Eve with cunning and guile.

And Eve - now fallen from God's grace
Did subdue Adam to his proper place.

Now they did know of good and evil
And both did live in Garden upheaval.

Now God did punish both Adam and Eve
To lives of solitude and servitude I do believe.

Pain at birth did she receive.
And he – sorrow unto death did God give.

And what is there to gain from this?
Does the serpent to the woman still hiss?

BILL RUSSELL

The Babe, knows everyone
Hit an everlasting homerun.

The Juice, on his quest to gain a mile
Stopped every beat and every dial.

The Golden Bear, may be the source
Of greatest wonders on the course.

The King, loved by all the common folk
Left all within his kingdom in puffs of smoke.

The Great One, with but mortal powers
Set the rink in the highest towers.

The Greatest, with a sting a wing and a rhyme
Became the greatest, the greatest of all time.

His Airness, made it so unfair
May still walk upon the air.

And Bill, ten fingers we know
And the other one on his toe.

THE AFRICAN-AMERICAN

Packed in rags as baggage
Onto galleons is the savage

Shipped to the land of the brave
And sold for a price is the slave

For nothing better and nothing bigger
He's destined to live his life as "nigger"

But Lincoln wrote and Lincoln hollered
Don't bind this man cause he's colored

Then along came Diamond Jack
And up did look this man who's Black

In song and rhyme and stage we know
The heart, the mind, the soul, the Negro

And now, as in fashion as Italian
Is that African-American

ISAAC AND THOMAS

Then there is Isaac and Thomas
Sons of a sister, so much a lass

Little Ike, every bit of five
As son and brother does he thrive

And Thomas, oh my oh my
I would, from now till I die

With infinite measures of silver
Give freely, for warming my shiver

With countless measures of gold
Send dearly, for comforting my cold

For the much Little Ike has given
Along with the love Tom has deep driven.

What Has This Pen?

What has this pen
To drip upon this page?
Who is this man
To think himself a sage?

And of this paper
What has it to say?
Is this some caper
To save another day?

Ink and sheet - the gall
To peruse every word
What care you all
If this poem is ever heard?

This is just a man
Trying to be brave
Asking what he can
Before they dig his grave

AND OF LOVE

And of love
What is there to say?
Who has not
Been touched this way?

Me - just once
But oh, so briefly in my life
Heart and spine
Still sentient of the knife

THE FOX HOLE

My foxhole gave a clear and almost
Perfect view of ambitions gone in
Disarray, of dreams taken in silence
By a cruel and desperate thief.

Completely unaware was I of that
Rogue that knew me well. Scope me out
Did he. Then - with tact, with patience,
With convenience did he attack.

My sensibilities, my soul, my being was
His aim. To drive me from my self
Was his goal.   With vigilance and with
Precision he sought to leave me

Stranded in complete confusion
And despair. And what was I to do?
When that unwanted foreigner comes
He comes to claim you for his own.

How indeed can one uncloak his well
Conceived disguise? Yes, there in that
Quaint and private little foxhole I was
Ready to cooperate completely with

My foe. To take me, time and time again
He would threaten. Don't you see, I am the
More clever, I am in control, I am the one
Who will not yield, he would say to me.

To drop me down and cover me up was
His intent. To confound my every
Thought, my every emotion, my every
Step was his ambition. Forget your

Bearings, he would utter in my brain.
Forget your bearings, I say, I will control
This being. Relate yourself to no one
Others have no clue what we're about.

You dream to be an architect do you?
A scholar on the subject you think, a
Historian of some sort - how senseless
You are. Between here and there you

Cannot even walk the line. Why peruse
Yourself away - every window will be
Broken, every door sealed, I will be
There to confiscate your every move.

You will be mine- in time you will be
Mine. Go ahead- place that M16
Below your chin. Qualify you expert
Or qualify oblivion. Stun the Cadre

Show them how irrelevant you and they
Are. Shatter your thoughts all over their
Well-pressed cammies. Drop an everlasting
Memory all over their highly polished boots.

Color the walls, color the ceiling, color
The floor, color them all in dreams
And aspirations, along with those
Nightmares and fantasies you haul.

WHITMAN AND WRIGHT

Whitman and Wright

Communicate with me.

Yes, dialogue, dialogue

Dialogue complete.

Keep me alive.

Beauty words and concrete

Emphatic contentment,

Elation and bliss arrive

Immortal, immortal

Whitman and Wright

I MET A MAN

I met a man in a restaurant
Who knew everybody
He knew the Governor
And his secretary
He knew the Mayor
And his secretary (Intimately it seemed)
He knew Mr. Jerry Jones
And Mr. Allan Jackson
This man in the restaurant
Had been everywhere too
He'd been to Spain
And to every Superbowl
It seemed
This man in the restaurant
Must have been very rich
To know everyone
And have been everywhere
This man in the restaurant
Seemed very hungry to me
So I bought him dinner

And left
Him to visit with and
Go wherever the hell
He wanted

YOU CAN NOT

YOU CAN NOT
READ OR WRITE

YOU CAN NOT
OWN A THING

YOU CAN NOT
MARRY YOUR LOVE

YOU CAN NOT
HAVE YOUR FREEDOM

YOU CAN NOT
DRINK THIS WATER

YOU CAN NOT
PLAY THIS GAME

YOU CAN NOT
ATTEND THIS SCHOOL

YOU CAN NOT
HAVE THIS SEAT

YOU CAN NOT
THINK TO VOTE

YOU CAN NOT
OWN THAT HOUSE

YOU CAN NOT
HONOR THAT MAN

YOU CAN NOT
HAVE THAT JOB

YOU CAN NOT
MARCH ON AND ON

THE NIGHT WALKER

The night's young
Thru her eyes
Her heart's cold
So she lies

Tellin' you 'bout
Your every look
Workin' to out
Your pocket book

The streets black
The lights alone
Come on Jack
Is her only moan

She's got to,
Got to get sold
Cause she ain't
Ain't gonna fold

CRICKETS

While the crickets are chirping
The cats are fiercely fighting
In the bushes outside
I suppose one of them
Is due his share of affection
But it seems clearly
His mate is not
Cooperating with the
Desired tenderness.

While the crickets are chirping
The dogs are barking
Wildly,   in a heated
Discussion of immense
Importance.

While the crickets are chirping
The teenagers are screaming
And laughing and screeching
Their tires
Honking and tooting
Their horns and playing
Their music in a somewhat
Seriously loud familiar Fashion.

While the crickets are chirping
The night is all quiet and
The chorus is complete.

SOMETHING PERMANENT

I drink alone
Every once in a while
I toss myself a bone
Too often I'm sure

It's a daily thing
And a nightly thing
But I don't want
To be gratified
For an instant anymore
Then it's over
I don't want to get high
Then it's done

I want something permanent.

I want to be a champion
But not a vagabond
Between championships

I don't want to get laid
Then it's done

I don't want to get rich
Then it's over

I don't want to get high
Again and again and again
I want something permanent.
I don't want to hear a song
That moves me
For a while
Then it's over

I don't want to hear a thought
That penetrates me
Then it's over
And done

I want something permanent;

Like what Adam had
Not just Eve
But all what
Adam had

Now...
How do I get there?

EVERYBODY LIVES ALONE

Everybody lives alone.
Lives alone
Dies alone
Comes and goes alone

Don't believe me
Well...

Try have someone else
Eat for you
Try have someone else's
Heart beat for you
Try have someone else
Walk for you

Every thought is personal
Every beat is internal

Yes...
You can make love with someone
They touch you
They hold you
They come with you
They laugh with you
They do the most intimate
Of things with you
Then you're alone
Again

You can share
All you want
But in the end
In the very end
You're alone

Don't believe me
Well…

Read this poem
Read this poem
Read this poem

Unless it's a thorn
That intimates you.
You're alone.

Unless you were born
Without a clue.
You're alone.

Unless you never mourn
When life's come due.
You're alone.

SLIPPING AWAY

I see the tears in her eyes
I hear the fear in her good-byes

She knows, beyond the words she'll talk
She goes, beyond the doors they'll lock

All those years together gone
We moved from the valley to the heights

It took us from dusk till dawn
I'd check the doors, the windows, the lights

We even graveled the lawn
If I wasn't there she wouldn't sleep nights

And disagreements, maybe one
But there were never, never any fights

> Take me home…
> I don't want to be here, she says
>
> Take me home…
> There must be other ways

Take me home…
I need to go work the days

Take me home…
To where my mother stays

I won't be here tomorrow
I'll find you wherever you go

Can one be so callow?
Seems unlikely, but yes, yes, it is so

Parting I say, is sad sorrow
There's nothing I can do, I know

What time I have, I borrow
Don't you dare, don't you dare go

I HAVE DIED
(MANY TIMES)

I have died
Many times
And every time
My soul stays with my body
It doesn't go anywhere
It just stays there
I cannot move
I cannot cover me with blankets
I cannot write something down
I cannot affect another person
I just cannot move
But I'm conscious
Of what's happening around me

I have died many times
And every time I feel no pain
I feel nothing
I'm just there
Waiting...

I have died many times
And each time I wait
Unable to do anything
Except think
And think
And wait...

I have died many times
That's how it is for me
I don't know how it will be for you
But the next time I die
I will wake up
And the time will come though
When I will not awaken
I will die
And I will wait...
Thinking...
Waiting...

I CAN TRAVEL FASTER

I can travel faster than the speed of light
I can think like no one ever has
Thought waves in my brain
Connect me with the Almighty
And guide me here and there

I can travel faster than the speed of light
I can die and un-die myself
I can think and un-think a thought
Time is not a problem either
I can un-time myself

I can travel faster than the speed of light
I did not inherit these abilities
I was grafted into my situation
It was my choice to take or leave
So I know I can do these things

I can travel faster than the speed of light
In fact, that's the least of my powers
I can go beyond the known universe
I can also go beyond the unknown
And I can take you with me

I can travel faster than the speed of light
You just have to listen carefully
Cautiously, as I intimidate you
Into my domain of being of existence
Where space and time are no more

I can travel faster than the speed of light
To a place where thought becomes
Where travel is not even a place
Not in the east or west, above or below
But within, definitely sunken within

I can travel faster than the speed of light
Where the physical doesn't matter
Where character takes shape
In the form of the un-physical
Where all will be equal

I can travel faster than the speed of light
Beyond wealth, poverty, illness, health
Beyond dreams, real or un-real
Beyond enemy, friend, relative, stranger
And there is such a place

I can travel faster than the speed of light
And there is no mystery to it
But you have to leave where you are
Completely and unequivocally leave
Accept no compromise just leave

I can travel faster than the speed of light
No money, no power, no fame
No sacrifice to leave what you don't have
Because what do you have – nothing
Because in this place there is nothing

I can travel faster than the speed of light
Yes, you live abundantly for a time
But a time is all you have
Why waste it so copiously
Travel with me faster than the speed of light

I can travel faster than the speed of light
I can go from where you are
At the speed of light I remind you
To where you want to be
Wherever that is

I can travel faster than the speed of light
Where does that get me going so fast?
To a place you've never been
To the place you're striving to get to
Day and night pushing to get to

I can travel faster than the speed of light
To that very same place you're going
With streets of silver and gold
Rivers with everlasting drinks of water
Mansions that everyone lives in

I can travel faster than the speed of light
The place I speak of doesn't fade away
The very same place I abide in now
My humble abode, my magnificent abode
Given me to graft another

I can travel faster than the speed of light
And my wings never tire of flight
In the rain, the wind or raging storm
And my wings never conspire
In passing to deceive or disguise

I can travel faster than the speed of light
And it's not a question of might
It's simply circumstance that mitigates
Between light speed and your speed
What the hell does that mean?

I can travel faster than the speed of light
Like I said I can travel so fast so fast
That my connections with the almighty
Guides me farther and faster
Than the speed of light

I can travel faster than the speed of light
I can, I can, You've just about seen me
Because your speed is not quite so fast
You will have difficulty comprehending
The speed at which I'm traveling

I can travel faster than the speed of light
I've gone as far as you can go today
Because at my speed there are no days
And night is not even an entity
Time is simply a non-existing realm

I can travel faster than the speed of light
How can that be possible?
Possible is where possible goes
And in my world it goes as faster
Than the speed of light

I can travel faster than the speed of light
What need is there for such velocity?
Who, besides me, wants this speed?
To travel so fast so far so often
With such ease and commitment

I can travel faster than the speed of light
In the domain I exclusively inhabit
There is no beginning or no ending
So let's bring this trip to a close
I suppose, at least as fast as the speed of light

I AM LOST

Thieves!
You stole red from red
Brown from brown
Made me naked
On your doorstep
Made me stagger
On broken glass
Kept me in backyards
Where my color fades
I am lost
The colors too bright
The spectrum too strong
I cannot leap
I cannot stretch
I cannot do so much.

www.ingramcontent.com/pod-product-compliance
Lightning Source LLC
Chambersburg PA
CBHW020242290526
45784CB00003B/1074